THE
OUTRAGEOUS
GUIDE
TO THE
WORLD CUP

THE AUTHORS

Paul Farrell is deputy editor of *The Phoenix*, and was previously with *Success Magazine*. A biochemistry graduate, he realised early that soccer — rather than the cell — is the basis of life as we know it. Although destined from birth to be a midfield general, he has opted instead for a totally sedentary lifestyle — due to a chronic lack of fitness. Described (by himself) as a great team player, Paul nevertheless respects the right of Eric Cantona to stroll around the pitch as if he owned it.

Graeme Keyes was born in Derry in 1961, which makes him — at 32 — still far too young to play for the national side. His only claim to footballing fame was to spend ten minutes in goal against an Eamon Dunphy selection at a charity match circa 1989 (dodgy knees). His first book, *Hung Like A Small Chicken*, sold well, and is still available at most good abattoirs throughout the country.

Keyes is a cartoonist for the *Irish Press, Evening Press, The Phoenix,* and *Private Eye.* His work has also appeared in the *Irish Independent, Sunday Press, The Guardian, Sunday Business Post, Cork Examiner, The New Statesman, The Pike, Irish Hardware, Irish Vintner, Squib, Yellow Press, The Cartoonist,* and *Dublin Opinion.*

To Fernando Hierro, who made this possible

THE OUTRAGEOUS GUIDE TO THE WORLD CUP

Paul Farrell   Graeme Keyes

THE O'BRIEN PRESS
DUBLIN

First published 1994 by The O'Brien Press Ltd.,

20 Victoria Road, Rathgar, Dublin 6, Ireland.

Copyright © *text* Paul Farrell *cartoons* **Graeme Keyes**

British Library Cataloguing-in-publication Data

A catalogue reference for this title is available from the British Library.

ISBN 0-86278-398-4

10 9 8 7 6 5 4 3 2 1

Cover illustration and design: Graeme Keyes

Typesetting and layout: Post Modern Tension. 6760474

Separations: Lithoset Ltd., Dublin

Printing: Colour Books Ltd., Dublin

SOME OF THE CARTOONS HEREIN HAVE APPEARED PREVIOUSLY

CONTENTS

WORLDCUP '94

INTRODUCTION

The World Cup is a serious business, but it doesn't have to be. *The Outrageous Guide to the World Cup* reaches the places other guides can't reach. This is it — everything you ever wanted to know about the World Cup, but never thought to ask.

Let Ray and Chips be your guides to USA '94, and travel onto the terraces and into the dressing rooms of Ireland's opponents in the World Cup. Get the inside story on Orlando and New York, and try your hand at Fantasy World Cup. What role did Saint Patrick play in the development of Irish soccer? What have Dave O'Leary and the second hand motor trade got in common? What brand of pen did Eamon Dunphy thrown down in disgust during Italia '90?

The answers are all here, along with a guide for World Cup bluffers, complimentary World Cup tickets, and much, much more …

USA '94 GETTING THERE

Once you have decided to enlist in Jack's Army, there are a number of steps that must be taken, and serious planning is required:

THE VISA There has been a lot of confusion in this area which it is now important to clarify. The visa in question is the documentation issued by the American Embassy to travellers from this and other third world countries. It is *not* — repeat *not* — the well known credit card. While a Visa card will come in handy in America, it will not get you through passport control. This is also true of Mastercard, and Diners Club, and American Express. These are old wives' tales and should be treated accordingly.

The visa in question is of the "multiple re-entry non-immigrant" class, known in Europe as the "Guinness visa". An intricate application form must be filled out, and this contains certain trick questions which should be answered carefully. For example where it asks (Q.7) if you have a criminal record for armed robbery and/or smuggling, it is advisable to answer in the negative in all circumstances. This is similarly true for Q.12 which asks if you were on or near the 6th floor of the Dallas Book Repository on November 22nd 1963. Also be sure to omit any references to membership — past or present — of the Nazi Party or the PDs.

MONEY If you follow the advice above, the way will now be clear to seek funding for your venture. Taking into account the price of World Cup match tickets, the whole trip should not cost more than £15,000. For some people this may require funding from an outside source such as a bank. Borrowing rather than robbery is advised here due to the

PASSPORT CONTROL

THE MAN WHOSE WORLD CUP ENDED IN SHANNON.

adverse effect an arrest will have on your chances of getting one of the all-important visas.

Borrowing the funds directly from a financial institution could prove an expensive business, so the best strategy here is the one adopted by the Irish team itself — sponsorship. By guaranteeing sponsors that you will have a good seat at the Irish

matches, they will happily pay you huge sums of money to display their logo on your shirt. The drawback here is that you cannot remove your shirt during the game like the rest of the fans who will therefore suspect that you are an accountant and refer to you through the whole of the tournament as "the tosspot". This problem will be compounded if other items of clothing are sponsored also.

WHAT TO PACK For long holidays this is often hard to judge, but in this case you will be indulging in a month-long orgy of soccer so the fashion options are rather limited — either the Irish team jersey plus jeans/shorts, or the Irish "away" jersey plus jeans/shorts. The latter is white with green trimmings and so will stain more easily than the predominantly green home strip. Hence a handy tip is to limit use of the away strip to special occasions.

Visitors to the USA often bring sausages and rashers, but since the World Cup lasts a full month it will be more effective to simply bring along a pig. Sedate it first to avoid trouble at customs.

SHANNON If you choose to fly direct from Ireland, you will have the added advantage of a trip to Shannon. What better way to start a holiday than in the wilds of Shannon Airport? Although only a short stop, there is much to see including the splendour of the arrivals hall and the natural beauty of the windswept departures lounge. The west of Ireland is renowned for its fishing and golfing, and although neither of these activities is possible in the airport, the experience — known locally as "the stopover" — is unlikely to be forgotten quickly.

RAY AND CHIPS TIP NO. 22
SPONSORSHIP

SOMETIMES THE ADVANTAGES OF GAINING
SPONSORSHIP SHOULD BE WEIGHED
AGAINST ONE'S STREET CREDIBILITY

DUTY FREE An essential part of any holiday, the duty free shop offers a wonderfully cheap and accessible range of alcohol and cigarettes. The trick here is not to be sidetracked by irrelevant items such as perfumes, chocolates and jewellery which eat into your refuelling time and duty free budget.

Warning: sweatshirts sporting shamrocks and leprechauns are cunningly placed around the store and may prove irresistible as you prepare to leave Irish soil. Do not under any circumstances be tempted — you will regret the hasty purchase as soon as you board the plane and are confronted by 300 similarly-clad passengers.

CUSTOMS One group of locals you will encounter at Shannon are the customs men and women of the United States government. This is not as dangerous as people have been led to believe, and indeed casualties are generally quite low, while fatalities are the exception rather than the norm. A handy way to convince the investigating officer that you intend to return home is to explain that you have set the timer on your video recorder. It is also a good idea to hide your supply of hard drugs in your pockets or better still plant them on some unsuspecting fellow passenger.

THE TRIP The most important thing to realise here is that there is a significant time difference between Ireland and America. Indeed, the USA has long been part of the 20th century, and you should therefore set your watch to American time as soon as you board the plane.

2

SEALBHÓIR   HOLDER   TITULAIRE (1)
Sloinne/Surname/Nom (2)

CONNELLY

Réamhainm Raedh/Forename(s)/Prénom(s) (3)

RAY, PADRAIG PEARSE JAMES

Náisiúntacht/Nationality/Nationalité (4)   Dáta breithe/Date of birth/Date de naissance (5)
Éireannach Irish Irlandaise   29/4/56

Gnéas/Sex/Sexe (6)   Áit bhreithe/Place of birth/Lieu de naissance (7)
M (IRELAND) DUBLIN

Dáta eisiúna/Date of issue/
Date de délivrance (8)

2 . 1 . 1986
As feidhm/Date of expiry/
Date d'expiration (9)

2 . 1 . 1996
Údarás/Authority/Autorité (10)

Oifig na bPasanna, Áth Cliath
Passport Office, Dublin

Ray Connelly
Síniú an tsealbhóra/Signature of holder/Signature du titulaire (11)

Airde/Height/Taille (12)   Dath na súl/Colour of eyes/Couleur des yeux (13)
169. cm   DEARG / RED

3

PAS A ATHNUACHAN
EXTENSION OF PASSPORT
PROROGATION DU PASSEPORT (14)

Bailíocht bhreise go dtí
Validity extended to
Validité prorogée jusqu'au (15)

Dáta/Date (16) ....

Bailíocht bhreise go dtí
Validity extended to
Validité prorogée jusqu'au (15)

Dáta/Date (16) ....

Bailíocht bhreise go dtí
Validity extended to
Validité prorogée jusqu'au (15)

Dáta/Date (16) ....

2

SEALBHÓIR   HOLDER   TITULAIRE (1)
Sloinne/Surname/Nom (2)

O'LOONEY

Réamhainm Raedh/Forename(s)/Prénom(s) (3)

GOBNAIT VIRGIL "CHIPS"

Náisiúntacht/Nationality/Nationalité (4)   Dáta breithe/Date of birth/Date de naissance (5)
Éireannach Irish Irlandaise   13/6/63

Gnéas/Sex/Sexe (6)   Áit bhreithe/Place of birth/Lieu de naissance (7)
M (IRELAND) CARLOW

Dáta eisiúna/Date of issue/
Date de délivrance (8)

26 . 6 . 1988
As feidhm/Date of expiry/
Date d'expiration (9)

26 . 6 . 1998
Údarás/Authority/Autorité (10)

Oifig na bPasanna, Áth Cliath
Passport Office, Dublin

Chips O'Looney
Síniú an tsealbhóra/Signature of holder/Signature du titulaire (11)

Airde/Height/Taille (12)   Dath na súl/Colour of eyes/Couleur des yeux (13)
190 cm   GORM / BLUE

3

PAS A ATHNUACHAN
EXTENSION OF PASSPORT
PROROGATION DU PASSEPORT (14)

Bailíocht bhreise go dtí
Validity extended to
Validité prorogée jusqu'au (15)

Dáta/Date (16) ....

Bailíocht bhreise go dtí
Validity extended to
Validité prorogée jusqu'au (15)

Dáta/Date (16) ....

Bailíocht bhreise go dtí
Validity extended to
Validité prorogée jusqu'au (15)

Dáta/Date (16) ....

GUIDE TO GROUP E

NORWAY

THE TEAM

PROBABLE LINE UP Christiansen; Pagansen; Erik Carlsen; Carl Eriksen; Erik the Viking; Samsen; Sen of Sam; Fjord Cortina; Harpoonsen; Quisling (may play for other side); Thor Hyerdahl; Thor Lowerdahl (substitute).

CHARACTERISTICS Very aggressive style and territorial in the extreme. The Norwegians generally adopt a version of the long ball game, called the longboat game, which involves sudden invasion into the opponent's half where they will often kidnap the goalkeeper.

WEAKNESSES Most effective on water or frozen surfaces so astroturf is unlikely to suit. If you give as good as you get the Norwegians can be surprisingly easy to stuff (see Brian Boru 1014 AD).

STRENGTHS The Norwegians should travel well to the USA — they have marvellous form away from home and indeed were unbeaten between 800 AD and 1000 AD. Florida is shaped a bit like Norway which may also help. Sometimes they are mistaken for the Finnish and so are not taken seriously by the opposition.

THE COUNTRY

HISTORY Very very violent, consisting mainly of rape and pillage in remarkably stylish (for their time) helmets. The first supreme ruler of Norway was King Harald the Fairhaired (872 AD), whose sexual proclivity led to the familiar saying, "whatever it is, Harald's had it". After centuries of kicking heads around Europe, Norway declared itself neutral in 1940 whereupon it was invaded by the Germans.

IRELAND V NORWAY (1014 AD) — HOME WIN

POLITICS The Vikings are the still the majority party although recently whales have been growing in popularity, especially with brown bread. There have been difficulties over Norway's entry into the EC because of its threat to harpoon Wales at the earliest possible opportunity.

CULTURAL ICON Henry Fjord — inventor of the inlet.

EUROVISION RECORD Appalling. One win (1985 in Sweden) and the record for coming last the most times, with "nul points" a familiar refrain from the judges. In fact this voting is simply revenge by Europe for centuries of aggro.

RELATIONSHIP WITH IRELAND Very poor since they got stuffed at Clontarf.

RELATIONSHIP WITH ENGLAND The Norwegians knocked them out of the World Cup and also beat them to the South Pole. However there is a grudging respect for English aggression and they have named their national airline after the SAS.

FAMOUS NORWEGIANS There aren't any, although Norwegians like to claim the god Thor as one of their own, but then so do Sweden, Finland, Denmark and Iceland. At one stage Ireland also tried to claim him under the grandparents rule.

THE POPE The only connection between the Vatican and Norway is Pope John Paul II's love of skiing.

FOOD Norwegians' favourite dishes include whale meat burgers, blubber bouillon, whale mousse, ox-whale soup, whale and chips (a Norwegian "one and one"). The abundance of cocktail sausages and fondue dishes can be explained by Norway's love of absolutely anything that has been pierced by a harpoon.

PLACES TO VISIT Norway is a huge open space and remarkably boring, which explains why the Vikings were always so anxious to travel. A measure of Norway's blandness can be gauged from the fact that the name Norway means "the way northwards" (this is true). It is however recommended that you visit Lillehammer — the scene of Torville and Dean's long-awaited come down and also Harding

THE SCREAM BY EDVARD MUNCH
(PORTRAIT OF AN EARLY FAN)

and Kerrigan's battle of wounded knee. Valhalla has proved a popular attraction, although mostly to Norse gods.

FANS

MELODY The Norwegians are not very melodious and tend to stick to numbers from popular Scandinavian musicals like "Viking and I". The famous whale mating songs are also popular, although most other countries find them intensely boring.

HOW TO SPOT THEM Most Norwegians wear woolly hats and gloves and all (including the women) have beards. The Norwegian flag is red and white and may be confused with the Red Cross. The way to tell them apart is that the Norwegians will be the ones firing the harpoons, not removing them.

WHAT THEY SAY Nothing of interest whatsoever.

QUESTIONS TO ASK What does a dead whale taste like? How long is a longboat? Where the hell is Lapland? What's the difference between a Norseman and a Viking? Why was Edvard Munch such a drip? Is there a Norwegian word for 'laugh'? How much is a krone worth anyway? What is there to do in Norway?

INSULTS "You've only won the Eurovision once"; "Remember Clontarf" (alternatively "one nil" or "Brian Boru is magic"); "All Scandinavians are the exact same"; "Aha are worse than Abba"; "Whales have feelings too"; "Long boats, short oars"; "Ibsen's really funny"; Any reference to Quisling.

MEXICO

THE TEAM

PROBABLE LINE-UP Bandito; Enchilada; Chihuahua; Guacamole; Poncho; Nacho; Tortilla; Tequila; Taco; Siesta; Chilli; Warmi (substitute).

CHARACTERISTICS As with all bandits, the Mexicans like to attack from the rear, using the element of surprise, and often they will place their team in the opponent's box before the kick off. The defenders are slow and lazy and always last out of the showers, hence the familiar term 'wetbacks'. Referees have to be diligent as the coin is often pocketed after tossing.

STRENGTHS On the left wing Speedy Gonzalez will prove especially difficult to pin down, while up front they have a dangerous bunch of mercenary sharp shooters known as the Magnificent Seven. The Mexicans of course will be no strangers north of the Rio Grande, and indeed they used to own large parts of the USA.

WEAKNESSES However, having lost New Mexico, Texas, and California, they are an unlikely bet to win the World Cup. The Mexicans have a well known tendency to take siestas during the game, and historically it is during this period that they concede many soft goals. They haven't actually won away from home since the Battle of the Alamo in 1836.

HISTORY The Mexicans used to be a very advanced civilisation until they discovered the sombrero. Before that the Aztecs — named after a once-popular Cadburys chocolate bar — built wonderful cities and lived in peace. This changed when the conquistadors arrived with very wide

FIVE MEXICAN BEERS... THREE TEQUILAS... TWO EXTRA HOT TACOS... WE CALL IT THE MEXICAN WAVE!

brimmed hats for the natives, turning them instantly into corrupt shifty bandits who talk through their noses and eat very hot and spicy foods. It also meant that hat stands had to be incredibly big in Mexico. In recent times Mexico has been in a constant state of revolution, and indeed, the national hero is revolutionary musician Frank Zappata.

POLITICS The controlling party is the Revolutionary Party, while the main right wing opposition parties include the Very Revolutionary Party and the Really Revolutionary Party. In the middle is the Fairly Revolutionary Party, while to the left are the Bandito Party and the No Good Rotten Bandito Party.

ECONOMICS Mexico is a rather poor country, especially compared with its neighbour, the USA. Indeed, the large difference in living standards north and south of the Rio Grande is known as the Gulf of Mexico.

CULTURAL ICON Poncho Villa — inventor of the poncho.

EUROVISION RECORD The worst of all group members, Mexico has never even entered the Eurovision, and indeed most Mexicans have never heard of Johnny Logan or Dana, which may explain their laid-back, somewhat carefree attitude.

RELATIONSHIP WITH IRELAND Irish people don't need a visa to visit Mexico. This is because there are absolutely no jobs whatsoever there.

FAMOUS MEXICANS John, Paul, George, Gringo.

ALCOHOL The Mexicans have a peculiar sense of humour and over the years have developed ingenious ways of using alcohol to make North Americans and Europeans look stupid. Hence you will see grown men trying to drink Mexican beer from a bottle bunged up with a slice of lime, or better still, drinking tequila with lemon and salt from a bottle that contains a dead worm.

FOOD Similarly, only a twisted sense of humour can explain burritos, enchiladas, re-fried beans and a variety of sauces designed to ignite the roof of your mouth, gut and stomach. The growing popularity of Mexican food around the world serves as a constant source of amusement in Mexico where it is only eaten because the locals can't afford anything else. The introduction of Tex-Mex food is the latest weapon in a war on taste buds worldwide, while Tortilla chips have recently started appearing at parties in Ireland, cunningly disguised as crisps.

However, the most audacious stunt to date by the Mexicans has been the mass export of their rats to North America and Europe under the name "chihuahua".

PLACES TO VISIT Mexico has a lot to offer the tourist (including Montezuma's Revenge) and, while the pyramids they leased from the ancient Egyptians are probably the most famous, there are many other spectacular attractions, although we can't think of any right now. Tourists often don't enjoy Mexico, and this was certainly the case with Leon Trotsky, whose murder there with an ice pick in 1940 effectively killed off Mexico's blossoming political asylum tourist industry. Earthquakes don't help either.

THE POPE As a Catholic country, Mexico is very popular with the Vatican. However, there has never been a Mexican pope because the cardinals, like most Mexicans, are generally not to be trusted.

FANS

MELODY Mexicans love to sing, although usually in an attempt to inflict pain on those around them.

HOW TO SPOT THEM No-one is easier to spot as they all wear sombreros and ponchos and travel in gangs behind a leader with a big moustache and a cigar, often terrorising small villages. They will also be the ones dancing around sombreros, kicking cuddly felines — a practice known as the Mexican cat dance. Their flag is the same colour as the Italians, but will be far more grubby.

WHAT THEY SAY They say things like "Hombre" and "Greeengo" through clenched teeth, and spit a lot. They also speak as if they have something very hot in their mouths, and often this is indeed the case.

QUESTIONS TO ASK Who invented the poncho and why? How long does a siesta last? Why does chilli sound cold but taste hot? Where's my wallet? How many times can you re-fry beans? What exactly is in a burrito?

INSULTS "You'll never win the Eurovision"; Only girls wear ponchos"; "Mexican food isn't fit for human consumption"; "Where the hell are the Aztecs?"; "Conquistadors are we".

ITALY

THE TEAM

PROBABLE LINE UP Lamborghini; Ravioli; Don Corleone; Tagliatelli; Alfa Romeo; Beta Romeo; Lambrusco; Paparazzi; Linguini; Gelatti; Frascati Superiore; Frascati Inferiore (substitute).

CHARACTERISTICS Spend a lot of time rolling around on the ground in agony and generally poncing about. Despite their camp appearance, they have a vicious side to their nature, and in the past opposing managers have been known to wake up with a horse's head in their bed. Early Italian teams honed their skills at the Colosseum where they practised against the Christians, and today the team still displays many of the traits picked up at that time.

WEAKNESSES Like all Italians the team spends far too much time on grooming and most carry small mirrors which can greatly affect their concentration. Notorious for their ability to surrender, all the Italian players carry a white flag.

STRENGTHS May have already bribed the referees.

THE COUNTRY

POLITICS There are three distinct political groups in Italy — fascists, communists and the mafia — the equivalent of the PDs, Democratic Left and Fianna Fáil respectively.

CULTURAL ICON Giuseppe Garibaldi — father of the Italian biscuit.

EUROVISION RECORD Very poor — one win (1990) in Yugoslavia when they pushed Ireland's Liam Reilly into second place … so they can't be all bad.

RELATIONSHIP WITH IRELAND Centres on the fish 'n' chips industry which they cornered here during the '60s with IDA assistance.

FAMOUS ITALIANS Michelangelo; Leonardo; Donatello; Raphael.

THE POPE The Italians fancy themselves as the only worthwhile popes and it sticks in their craw that the current occupant is a Pole. The most famous Italian pope was Victor Borgia, who went on to make it big in Hollywood.

FOOD Pasta is the potato of Italy and Italians cannot survive without it for more than 24 hours. Pasta comes in many shapes, none of them sensible. Spaghetti, for example, looks and tastes like straw, but is much harder to get into your mouth. When the first Italian emigrants to reach Ireland asked for pasta they were misunderstood and were given batter instead, and the very first Gino's take-away opened the next day. There is a saying in Italy that at the table no-one grows old — this is actually untrue. At the table no-one grows thin.

THE FANS

MELODY One of the favourite songs of the Italian fans is the familiar "O Sole Mio" which they ripped off the Cornetto advert. Pavarotti numbers are very popular on the terraces but Vivaldi is the darling of the Italian fans, especially "The Four Seasons", which is named after a popular pizza.

FASHION The toga is the quintessential Italian garment and was introduced by Benetton in 23 BC.

However, the advertising campaigns caused outrage in ancient Rome, particularly the one — entitled "Beware the Ides of March" — which showed Julius Caesar's blood-splattered toga. The "Christians at the Colosseum" was another high profile Benetton campaign which managed to capture the public imagination.

WHAT THEY SAY As with most continentals, the Italians speak very quickly and are difficult to understand. However familiar phrases include "Mama Mia" (oh shite); "Don Corleone" (you're dead); "Ave un Papa" (the referee's a bastard); "Spaghetti carbonara" (we'll see you all outside). The familiar form of address is "ciao" (pronounced chow) which means both hello and goodbye, hence the old saying "the Italians don't know whether they're coming or going". This is also used to explain their renowned ability to retreat during World War II.

HOW TO SPOT THEM They are very emotional and cry a lot, especially when they lose, win, or draw. However, those carrying violin cases are in general not to be messed with. The men grab their crotch a lot to show they are great lovers — and to check that it's still there.

INSULTS "You've only won the Eurovision once" (alternatively "Five:One" repeated); "Benetton ads are a load of bolognese" ; "The Pope is from Poland"; "Tangentopoli" (repeat three times to the tune of 'Here we go'); "Italian cars have crap gear sticks"; Any reference to World War II.

"HEY! NICE TOUCH LUIGI!"

GUIDE TO THE IRISH VENUES

THE BIG (GREEN) APPLE.

ORLANDO

WHERE TO FIND IT Located on the outskirts of Disney World.

GETTING THERE The cheapest and quickest route is via Euro Disney. It is a little known fact that Disney World, Disney Land and Euro Disney are all linked by magic tunnels.

WEATHER Florida is called the "sunshine state". Unlike Ireland, the Americans take the trades description act very seriously, hence the range of weather here is rather limited. Hawaiian shirts are *de rigueur* resulting in the famous day-glo hue of the whole state.

PEOPLE The locals are animated, consisting mostly of Disney characters such as Mickey Mouse. Further south there is an increasing number of the very old or nearly dead, due to a tendency among wrinkly Americans to come to Florida to see out their last days. This preponderance of the undead explains why Florida is sometimes called the "hospice state".

THINGS TO SEE The most popular tourist attraction for the Irish in recent years has been the *Ben Dunne Shrine*, located on the 17th floor of the Grand Cypress Hotel. For just $10 you get to sit on the famous window ledge as well as try out the spacious bath (fits two). Ask at the hotel for details on 'Escorts in a Flash'. Other attractions include *Disney World* — the original, and a long way from the Euro Disney disaster (as with the World Cup, there is absolutely no French input here). The famous *Key Largo* is another popular haunt, although remember — it is already available on video at home.

WHAT TO EXPECT Fans will be greeted by a number of battalions of heavy armoured vehicles. These were recently ordered by Sheriff Kevin Bearry who got the wrong end of the stick when he was told that Jack's Army was on its way. Certain to prove a problem for the green and white army, it

would appear to be no coincidence that he is the sheriff of Orange County.

WHAT TO AVOID NASA Space Shuttle rides from Cape Canaveral — strictly for risk takers; Alligators — more dangerous than bungy jumping; Orange County — unwelcoming (see above); Miami — although it attracts many tourists every year, most of them leave in a box. A familiar phrase in Miami is "I've got a magnum in my pocket" — do not take this to be an invitation to a champagne dinner for two. It should also be recalled that Al Capone died here from syphilis in 1947.

NEW YORK

WHERE TO FIND IT Beside the Statue of Liberty — a gift from the French, who got Euro Disney in return. They now want to swop back.

GETTING THERE Most people only get to New York by mistake.

PEOPLE There are two types of people in New York — muggers and victims (or tourists as they are sometimes called). The way to tell them apart is that the tourist is the one lying face-down in the street.

WHAT THEY SAY "Stick 'em up!"

WHAT THEY WEAR Bullet-proof vests.

WHAT TO SEE Greenwich Village is the Temple Bar of New York, but without the tax breaks. Don't visit between 2pm and 3pm, when the locals are very selfish. This is known as "Greenwich Mean Time". Broadway — or "the way of the broads" — is a famous gathering point for New York women. They are, however, remarkably reserved, hence the song line: "If I can make it there, I'll make it anywhere".

WHAT TO AVOID The streets. If you must, walk on the sunny side of the street — this increases your chances of survival, and you might get a tan. The best way to avoid being mugged is to simply leave your money in Ireland. There is absolutely no point in acting tough — even King Kong got whacked in New York City.

GETTING ABOUT Try the subway if you have a death wish. Otherwise New York taxis will take you anywhere, except where you want to go. However it's not the driver's fault that he can't speak English.

WHERE TO STAY The Waldorf Astoria comes highly recommended. Rates begin at $1,200 per night. The splendid "Dick Spring Suite" is far more expensive.

RAY AND CHIPS TIP NO. 262

DON'T WAVE AT A NEW YORKER'S GAL...
ESPECIALLY WITH YOUR TONGUE!

PADDY'S DAY New York is known as the "Big Apple" or "Big Fruit", much to the annoyance of the Ancient Order of Homophobes. They have threatened to cancel the annual Saint Patrick's Day parade because of a plans to have it moved to the borough of Queens.

NB The football stadium is actually located in East Rutherford, New Jersey, a nondescript state famous only for Atlantic City — the Bray of the USA. Bruce Springsteen came from New Jersey, but never went back.

... IT IS WORTH NOTING THAT NEW YORKERS ARE FAMED FOR THEIR BLUNTNESS AND IT IS ADVISABLE FOR VISITORS TO DEVELOP A SOMEWHAT THICK SKIN

"WELL, WELL, WELL, IF IT ISN'T MISTER SKIDMARKS!"

COMPLIMENTARY WORLD CUP TICKETS

THE UNITED STATES OF AMERICA
A Beginner's Guide

HISTORY

The United States of America used to be owned by the Red Indians, but today is split roughly 50:50 between the Japanese and Coca Cola. US historians have concentrated on the cowboys from the Wild West, to the detriment of the pigboys, sheepboys and henboys from the Timid North, Mild East, and Soft South respectively. The henboys were also remarkably philosophical, hence the phrase "Deep South", still in common usage.

POLITICS

Abraham Lincoln is the most famous American president, and it is said of him that he never once told a lie, but this was long before the advent of congressional hearings. Judging by the recent past, it can safely be assumed that "Honest Abe" told a few whoppers in his time. The current president is a cat called "Sox".

THE IRISH CONNECTION

It was actually Saint Brendan who discovered America, but the Spanish fishing fleet — miles outside their own waters as usual — took all the credit. Renowned Irish American sports stars include John F. Kennedy, who is best remembered today for his tendency to go offside, but was at his

best playing away from home. His brother, Ted Kennedy, tried his hand at motor sports but some particularly careless driving cut short a promising career. Famous Irish American politicians include L.B. Johnson (who founded a bakery in Dublin with Mooney and O'Brien), and the man with the worst hairdo on Capitol Hill — Tip Head O'Neill.

GEOGRAPHY

A vast country, most of America is highly dangerous, the exceptions being the independent republics of Disneyland and Graceland. There are certain counties in the Midwest renowned for bitter sarcasm, known as the dry counties. The most common feature on the roads is the greyhound. Unlike in Ireland, greyhounds are used as a method of transport by much of the population, a rather inhumane practice which the anti-coaching lobby is determined to have banned.

CULTURE

America is often described as a "cultural melting pot", which when translated means there are riots on a regular basis. The serial killer is one of the more acceptable American cultural phenomena (especially when compared with the Hula-Hoop and skateboard), but this is to be expected in a country where the "Saturday night special" is not an RTE chat show hosted by Pat Kenny, but instead a small, deadly handgun.

FOOD

America is the home of fast food, an abbreviation of "fasting food" — so-called because it has the same dietary content as a fast. Typical American dishes include the hot dog, which is not a Chinese delicacy, but something far more disturbing. The potato — sometimes spelled "potatoe" in America — comes in a variety of disguises, most disgustingly hash browns. Be warned, a hash cake has nothing to do with potatoes.

ALCOHOL

Alcohol is taken seriously, and there is a TV programme — called *Cheers* — entirely devoted to the subject. The process of imbibing the product differs greatly from the Irish experience and can involve sprinkling it on the testicles ("on the rocks"), or forcing it down the throat ("by the neck"), while standing to attention ("straight up"). As in a hospital, you can also get "shots" in most American bars. (You can also get shot in most American bars, but that's another story.)

LANGUAGE

Although the Americans claim to speak English, this is not true. They speak Spanish or "American", a form of English often heard on TV programmes. This can prove confusing, and in America, Ray and Chips would be called Ray and Fries. Chips are not chips, chips are crisps — get the picture? The Americans do not have lifts, they have elevators. They do not give lifts, they give rides. Therefore if asked: "Do you fancy a ride?", don't get too excited. They do not wear trunks, rather they have trunks in their cars, where we have boots. Hence American soccer fans have been known to shout: "Put the trunk in" during competitive matches.

SPORTS

The Americans can't play soccer, and prefer American Football, which is simply sumo wrestling with lots of padding. The most famous team is the Miami Dolphins, where Flipper is the established quarterback. Baseball is actually more boring than cricket, though not as boring as the Norwegians. The players try to liven things up by adopting names like "Babe Ruth", which in Ireland would lead to some awful slagging on the terraces. The Americans also take basketball seriously.

TED KENNEDY TAKES A SHOT AT GOAL...

THE WORLD CUP A USER'S GUIDE

A BRIEF HISTORY

Once upon a time countries used to come together on a regular basis for the purpose of knocking the stuffing out of each other, a sport that became known as world war. It proved so popular than a couple of Frenchmen bought the franchise, and applied it to the far more violent sport of soccer. The result was an organisation called FIFA (Football Is Fairly Appealing).

Since then the World Cup has grown to be the biggest single sporting event in the world after the Eurovision Song Contest, which is of course a far more violent affair altogether.

THE WINNERS

As a rule the winning country is always Germany, or her World War II ally, Italy. England is the exception that proves the rule. Germany is the only country ever to have started two world wars, won the Eurovision with a song about peace, and won three World Cups. Their most famous victory was achieved over France when the canny French placed a line of men across the half way line, only for the Germans to walk around them. This line is today known as the "Maginot Line", which when translated means "queue of dozy Frenchmen".

It is no coincidence that Germany's WW II partners — Italy — also have managed to notch up three World Cup victories, while the Allies could only manage one victory between the lot of them. This 6:1 result proves that the chances of winning a world war are inversely proportional to the chances of winning the World Cup. The only other winners of the trophy have been the South American countries, all of which are notable asylums for fleeing Nazis.

THE NO-HOPERS

Recent times have seen an explosion in the popularity of soccer in countries that were never meant to play the game and who are just making up the numbers — nil being the most common one. These countries have helped ensure their certain failure by developing their very own rules to make the oldest game in the world "more exciting":

CAN WE HAVE OUR BALL BACH?

JAPAN The sports-mad Japanese are a proud people and anything less than victory is unthinkable. Tied games are therefore decided by the "sudden death" play-off. In the country which gave us kamikaze pilots and hara-kiri, the "final" whistle is taken quite literally, and both teams draw huge swords on which they ceremoniously impale themselves out of a sense of shame.

AMERICA The Americans have replaced extra time with the "shoot-out", where both sides arm themselves with Colt 45s and let rip. The game at the OK Corral is still remembered as a classic of its type. "Offside" is another concept the Americans have trouble with, as they believe that their Constitution guarantees the right to be exactly where you want to be when the ball is delivered. This particular ruling is currently the subject of a Supreme Court appeal by the vociferous anti-choice lobby.

AUSTRALIA This is a country that calls its national team the "Socceroos", which speaks for itself really. Australian soccer differs from FIFA's rules in that all the players carry a tin of lager which is constantly refilled during the game. When a game is tied (there are rarely any goals scored) there follows a massive punch-up in which everyone enjoys himself thoroughly. If the teams are not level, the outcome is the same.

AFRICA The Africans are actually very good at soccer, but they can't afford footballs and this has greatly hindered their progress to date. The success in 1990 of Cameroon is still a mystery, but then so is Norway's 1985 Eurovision victory.

THE QUALIFIERS FOR USA '94

Apart from the hosts, the holders, and the teams in Ireland's group, USA '94 plays host to 18 other qualifying countries which have paid in blood, sweat, and intensive sponsorship negotiations to display their assorted logos on the world stage:

ARGENTINA Likely to miss Maradona who has been busy missing members of the press, but only by a couple of inches.

BELGIUM Should stick to chocolates.

BOLIVIA Fairly near Brazil.

BRAZIL The home of Pele, whose real name is actually very long.

BULGARIA The only qualifier to have named its capital city after Sofia Loren.

CAMEROON Almost an anagram of macaroon.

COLOMBIA This team is unlikely to make it through US customs.

GREECE Gave the world moussaka but got away with it.

MOROCCO Casablanca is home of the replay — hence "play it again, Sam".

NETHERLANDS The only team reclaimed from the sea.

NIGERIA Often confused with Algeria.

ROMANIA Fans should keep a close eye on goalkeeper Dracula, who is very poor under crosses.

SAUDI ARABIA Will attempt to convert opposition to Islam early in the first half.

SOUTH KOREA Like North Korea, but not as dangerous.

SPAIN Helped Ireland keep Denmark at home, so they're OK.

SWEDEN See Norway.

SWITZERLAND Happier on skis.

"LOOKS LIKE HE'S GOING FOR THE OLD **4-4-2** FORMATION."

THE POLITICALLY CORRECT GUIDE TO SOCCER

Soccer is a sport littered with politically incorrect terms which, long overdue, are now to be excluded from use. These include:

BALL Ridiculously masculine in nature, the ball will be replaced with the more acceptable term GLAND.

CAMP Homophobic term for the team base which has no part to play in the modern game. To be replaced by LOCATION.

HOME GROUND As many people are today homeless, this is unnecessarily insensitive and shall be replaced by NEARBY GROUND.

JERSEY A breed of cow, which is a highly derogatory term for a woman. It will be replaced by BLOUSE.

MANAGER An obviously sexist term aimed at undermining all women. It is to be replaced by the term PERSONAGER. The word "son" will be removed from this at a later date.

PASS Unacceptable in the work place, making a pass will now be forbidden on the soccer pitch. In future, players will DIRECT the gland.

SCORE A vulgar term for sexual conquest, it is remarkable that such a word has survived so long. Players will no longer "score" but ACHIEVE A GOAL.

SHORTS To be replaced by VERTICALLY CHALLENGEDS.

STRIP Derived as it is from the term "strip show", such a word has no place in the modern game. Players will now wear MATCHING OUTFITS.

WINGER Contains the word "win" which is no longer the purpose of the game, rather it is the taking part that counts. Hence the new term COMPETER.

ON THE PITCH

Other changes in the game will see players wearing letters rather than numbers, which will ensure all players feel equal as nobody will have a higher number than anyone else. Goalkeepers are said to be particularly pleased with this introduction.

In order to take some of the nastiness out of soccer, opposing teams should be sure to give each other a fair chance. If, for example, someone is sent off, then the other team should remove one of their players as promptly as possible.

All teams should have at least one visually challenged member, and age should under no circumstances be taken into consideration when picking a team. Indeed the total absence of players over 50 years old has been of great concern to the authorities, although the Irish team at least has been helping to turn the tide in this area.

ON THE TERRACES

The fans will in future behave in a far less partisan manner, and cheer for both teams equally. This will remove intimidation and harassment from the pitch, and contribute to a healthier environment. Similarly, chants such as "You're worse than San Marino" will be replaced by the more acceptable

"Although you're losing at the moment, don't give up, things can only get better". "Bring on the dustbins" can only be chanted at the end of the game when cleaning up begins.

Under no circumstances can there be any references to the referee's allegedly questionable parentage. It is however permitted to refer to Eamon Dunphy as "an irresponsible driver".

"FOUL HIM?!? NO, NO, I WAS MERELY ENABLING HIS HORIZONTAL COMMUNION WITH MOTHER EARTH!"

USA '94 LEXICON

An explanation of some words and phrases you may come across during the World Cup:

BRIT *n* one who misses out on huge sporting occasions: *Graham Taylor is a complete brit*

BRUTON *n* highly ineffective right winger: *I wish they'd sell that bruton before we get relegated*

CHARLTON *vb* **1.** to scowl menacingly at those with whom you disagree. **2.** to earn ridiculously large amounts for after-dinner speeches

DODGY KNEES *n* another term for a hangover: *Jaze, I had too much to drink last night and woke up with an awful pair of dodgy knees*

DUNPHY *vb* **1.** to gesticulate or drive in an erratic manner: *Look out, that taxi is dunphying all over the road.* **2.** to throw a pen in a violent or aggressive manner

GILES *n* a knowledgeable but intensely dour person (usu. with appalling hair style): *I thought the giles in the corner would never leave*

KEANE *n* very expensive item originating from Cork — sometimes *roy keane* to differentiate from *terry keane* (one who gossips)

MAGEE *vb* to expose one to endless irrelevant trivia — *I was almost mageed to death listening to him last night*

MORAN *n* very old and given to breaking down (gen.

used in second-hand motor trade): *that damn car you sold me was a moran* (see also *o'leary*)

O'HERLIHY *n* **1.** one who is unable to open a bottle of champagne. **2.** *adj* bubbly

TICKET *n* rare and incredibly expensive object, thought to be mythical.

JACK SUPPORTING AN OPEL

OPEL SUPPORTING A JACK

DOSH

LET'S PLAY FANTASY WORLD CUP

Fantasy Football is the latest craze to hit the game of soccer, allowing layabouts and armchair experts around the country to manage their own top-level team. Now you get the chance to try your skills at Fantasy World Cup.

HOW TO PLAY

1. PICK A COUNTRY Hint: try Germany.

2. CHOOSE A MANAGER Hint: don't pick Graham Taylor.

3. NEGOTIATE A SPONSORSHIP DEAL As in real World Cup soccer, this is a minefield of legal technicalities and there are certain points you should bear in mind:

Pick an established company that will be around after the tournament ends, and beware of companies that make outlandish promises such as free flights to America with the purchase of any of their products. Stay clear of controversial companies whose adverts aim to shock. Posters of blood splattered team jerseys are not necessarily the image a national team wants to portray, although it may be all right for Wimbledon FC. Some names are simply not suitable for national team sponsorship, including Semtex, Kalashnikov, British Nuclear Fuels, and Union Carbide.

Warning: If you pick the Irish team, avoid leading brands of contraceptives. Although an ideal sponsor for a team with a strong defence, contraceptives will cause controversy at home and lead to tabloid headlines like: *IT'S OFFICIAL — JACK'S LADS ARE ON THE PILL!!*

4. PICK A FORMATION The formation you choose will dictate the type of game your team will play — for example the long ball game favoured by Jack Charlton, or simply the spherical one used by most teams. Traditional formations include: 4 - 2 - 4; 4 - 3 - 3; and 4 - 4 - 2. With Fantasy World Cup however, the options are limitless and you are not confined to ordinary numbers. A variety of mathematical functions are available, and one popular formation is: $2\pi/6 - \sum 4x - \int\sqrt{2\Omega}$.

5. DESIGN THE KIT Fantasy World Cup doesn't limit you to the kits usually worn by the country you pick. Choosing the right colours and coordinating them is very important — the records show that brown, for example, not only lacks aesthetic appeal but has never been worn by a World Cup winning team. This is also true of cerise, maroon and other derivations of purple. Take care to ensure that the shirts, shorts and socks don't clash, unless playing against the fashion-conscious Italians — it will put them off their game completely.

6. COMMISSION A SONG Fantasy World Cup allows you have your World Cup song written by the middle-of-the-road songwriter of your choice. Just imagine having the team song written by Phil Collins, or Johnny Logan! Maybe you want Chris de Burgh — you got him. The options are literally endless.

7. BEGIN Simply fill in your choices and then imagine what would happen during the tournament. Use a pencil, and if you're not happy with the result, simply rub out your original choices and start again.

MY TEAM ....

MY MANAGER.......................................

MY SPONSOR ....

MY FORMATION ....

MY KIT ....

FANTASY FOOTBALL CARTOON

A BLUFFER'S GUIDE TO USA '94

You may have missed out on Euro '88 and Italia '90, but here's your chance to sit in any pub in the country during USA '94 and pontificate with the best of them.

HANDY TIPS

The World Cup is a trophy awarded every four years to Germany. There is no such thing as the World Saucer. Everybody in the country has claimed they were in the Nekar Stadium on June 12th 1988 to see Ray Houghton put the ball in the English net. However, do not claim that you saw the Irish team perform at the Dandelion Market for 50p before they were famous — this is for U2 bluffers only.

THE PITCH

You will often hear the cry of: "Get the ball in the box ya dozy gobshite". There is in fact no box on the pitch — it is just a two-dimensional parallelogram adjacent to the goal. Geometry is never taken seriously by football supporters — hence meaningless phrases such as the "square ball".

MARADONA

The name Maradona will crop up during the tournament, and there will be plenty of references to a recent loss of form, and trouble with drugs and the press. Never say: "I loved *Like a Virgin*".

METAPHORS

Metaphors with which you should be familiar
include: "Sick as a parrot" (Translation: "We lost").
This is species-specific and cannot be replaced with,
for example: "Sick as a budgie". "Over the moon"

*"— YES JOHN. PUTTING T'BALL BEHIND
T'MAN DOES INCLUDE T'GOALIE..."*

(Translation: "We won") is also specific and cannot be replaced with other astronomical references. The encouraging shout of: "On your bike son" (Translation: "Shift your arse") is never substituted with: "On your racer/skateboard, etc". Also be aware that in World Cup competition, an Irish draw is considered a win.

THE REFEREE

Never ask: "Who does the guy in black play for?". This is the referee. He is there only as a target for the fans' verbal abuse. It is recommended that regularly throughout the game you shout something vile about the referee and his father. His eyesight is also always questionable — hence the familiar cry of: "Blind bastard". Warning: The referee is always referred to as "the ref" or "bastard". The word "referee" only occurs in songs such as *Who's your father, referee?*

THE PLAYERS

There are 22 players on the pitch, including the two goalkeepers who wear very colourful jerseys to differentiate them from their colleagues. Never say: "Oh, I just love his top". Warning: The goalkeeper is always referred to as "the keeper", or "the goalie", never the goalkeeper — this is a dead giveaway. A "dangerous" player is one who may score against Ireland, not one with a criminal record for aggravated assault. "Good in the air" has nothing to do with being a frequent flyer, while a "dribbler" doesn't have problems controlling the flow of saliva from his mouth.

THE HOT SEAT

Although you have never managed a top-level football club, it is OK to suggest that you could have picked a better side than Jack Charlton (always "Big Jack") did. If Ireland lose a game, immediately point out that: "Jack couldn't pick apples in an orchard, never mind a World Cup team". You will receive knowing nods from hard-core fans.

Similarly, although you have never played top-level soccer, it is perfectly legitimate to suggest that you — or indeed your granny — could have scored that one Aldo missed early in the first half (Note: "Aldo" is John Aldridge).

OFFSIDE

Offside is a difficult concept, and bluffers should not enter into discussions on the subject. However watch out for phrases like: "They're playing the offside game". This is a reference to a team's defensive strategy, so do not reply: "I thought they were playing soccer". Similarly, the "offside trap" is not a piece of equipment for capturing offsides.

DO NOT SAY

"Where's Liam Brady?"; "When do we get to play them at home?"; "That Eamon Dunphy's very good"; "Any chance of the Triple Crown?"; "The referee was very good at spotting our indiscretions".

DO SAY

"It was a game of two halves"; "We were beaten by the woodwork"; "It's not a patch on Italia '90"; "Olé, Olé, Olé"; "Paul McGrath's a great player"; "It was Hierro who got us here".

70

GAY BYRNE

PUBLISHERS NOTE: Gay Byrne actually has nothing specific to do with the World Cup. This is is just a cheap attempt by the authors to get a mention on his radio show!

FROM SAINT PATRICK TO JACK CHARLTON

Irish soccer under Jack Charlton has evolved greatly from rather humble beginnings:

SAINT PATRICK Like Jack Charlton, Saint Patrick came from across the Irish Sea and brought with him his own ideas about how the game of football should be played, concentrating on getting the ball behind the man. This style was adopted by other Celtic sides, notably Jock Stein's Glasgow team of the 1970s. Saint Patrick had no time for fancy or "slippery" players, all of whom he banished from the national squad.

BRIAN BORU The first successful Irish manager was Brian Boru. His most memorable victory was achieved over the Norwegians at the FAI's new ground in Clontarf in 1014. It was a controversial game with the Norwegians complaining that they had been robbed (a rather ironic claim for Norsemen at that period in history) and that the deciding goal was offside. To this day they haven't forgotten the result, and neither have the Irish.

STRONGBOW In the 12th century Irish soccer was shaken up with the arrival of Strongbow, a no-nonsense foreigner, again very much in the Jack Charlton mould. He introduced many aspects of the Norman game still evident here today, and brought with him a team of Norman advisers (including Norman Wisdom, Norman Schwarzkopf, and Norman Bates) who settled quickly into the Irish way of life.

MANY OF FOOTBALL'S MOST ARDENT FANS ARE WOMEN — ALTHOUGH SOME ATTITUDES DIE HARD

These Normans became "more Irish than the Irish themselves", and soon their offspring were playing for the national team. This is thought to be the first example in Irish soccer of what was to become known as the "grandparents rule".

THE PALE The 16th century saw the growing influence of the English Football Association here, which began with the establishment of the Pale. This was a coaching school where many of the Irish traits were removed from the game and replaced with a concentration on the English (high ball) game.

FEUDAL FOOTBALL Outside the Pale new laws were introduced which saw a change from the old Brehon system — whereby a team's ground was owned by the tribe and elected chief (fans and manager) — to a feudal system which saw all power vested in a chairman.

PLANTATIONS The successful plantation of Ulster had a serious effect as many of Ireland's star players had come from the Ulster clubs, including the great centre forward Hugh O'Neill (or Red Hugh as he was sometimes known because of his fanatical support for Manchester Utd.). There were now two Irish sides, kicking with different feet, and inevitably this led to some fierce local derbies where both managers regularly exchanged four-letter words — a tradition still carried on today.

OLIVER CROMWELL A succession of poor managers resulted in a series of humiliating home defeats, most notably at the hands of Oliver Cromwell's team, whose Wimbledon-style tactics proved too tough for the demoralised green army. William of Orange also inflicted notable defeats on the Irish, although the poor conditions (for July) at the Boyne ground were a factor on the day.

PENAL LAWS The introduction of the Penalty or Penal Laws, ensured Irish defeats for years to come by preventing any Irish team from having its own goalkeeper or wearing football boots. As a result it was difficult to find enough players to make up a full team, and the FAI called for anyone with an interest in the game to sign up. This team was known as the Irish Volunteers.

THE CANTONA FACTOR In the 18th century the Irish football authorities signed a deal with the French Football Association in a bid to stop the rot. Although the French did try to send over a team of experienced coaches, they never arrived due to some very nasty weather at Bantry Bay. Meanwhile they had become more concerned with the introduction of major changes in their own game — a period known as the French Revolution.

THE GREAT FAMINE In the middle of the 19th century the Irish team went through its longest period without a victory, a time known by the die-hard supporters as the Great Famine. The establishment of the Irish League however proved a popular move, and was accompanied by a new youth policy called Young Ireland.

The 20th century saw the introduction of laws stating that the home team always got to kick off and choose which way it played. This was known as Home Rule.

DEV In 1916 the busy Easter schedule saw some major upsets, particularly in Dublin. Eamon de Valera was then appointed manager, and once again opted for the long ball game, hence "the Long Fellow".

JACK CHARLTON Jack Charlton's reign is remembered for his decision to introduce new blood into the squad, most of it foreign. The success of his Irish team increased proportionately as the amount of Irish blood decreased.

THE FUTURE By the middle of the next century there will be no Irish blood in the national squad, by which time the team will be more Irish than the Irish themselves.

UG, THE INVENTOR OF THE POPULAR
(IF BRIEF) SPORT OF FOOT ROCK

AFTER ONLY MODERATE SUCCESS AS A STRIKER
BOB FINALLY FOUND HIS FORTE IN GOAL

THE JACK CHARLTON STORY

THE EARLY DAYS Big Jack started off life as Little Jack, and in between spent some time as Medium Jack. Growing up in Northumberland, it was inevitable that he would find himself down the mines like his father. His grandfather managed to avoid the pits by heading for Hollywood and making it big under the name Charlton Heston.

Medium Jack's no-nonsense approach to mining resulted in greatly increased coal output, especially from old mines that were considered over the hill. However, some miners found his style too workmanlike.

THE FOOTBALLER As Big Jack, he was far too tall to go down the mines, and opted instead for a career in football, having previously had an adventure involving a beanstalk that left him a little shaken. On the football pitch he was easy to spot in his familiar cloth cap and fishing gear. Big Jack was not averse to using his height advantage, or his studs, and was renowned for putting opposing forwards under "pressure" — a footballing term for "doctor's care". With Norman "bites your legs" Hunter, he formed a partnership more feared than the Kray Twins.

THE MANAGER At Leeds United he played under Don Revie, who taught him everything he knew about soccer. This suggests that any day now Big Jack will piss off to Saudi Arabia, although lucrative sponsorship deals could possibly keep him here. As a manager he developed his now-familiar style of

getting the ball behind the man, rather than in the net. After 13 years with glamour sides like Middlesborough, he landed the Irish job, the main

TWACK !!!!

attraction being the abundance of well-stocked rivers and potential sponsorship deals.

THE IRELAND JOB Big Jack succeeded Eoin Hand as manager of the Irish team, so nothing whatsoever was expected of him. Looking at his squad he immediately noticed what was wrong — the complete absence of foreign players. While this has proved a drawback to the managers of all other national sides, Big Jack simply opted to find some decent foreigners, and then picked their Irish grandparents for the team.

Although this strategy did introduce some much-needed new blood, it has also resulted in a very old squad. The average age of an Irish player is now 57, although the likes of Kevin Moran and David O'Leary are much older than this. Indeed, each international match is considered a possible testimonial by the whole team. It is not surprising that some of Ireland's best results were achieved last year, during the European Year for the Aged.

WHAT HE WEARS Anything that he is sponsored to wear.

LIKES Monaghan Milk, Shreddies, the Bank of Ireland, the *Sunday Press*, and anybody else who will put their hands in their pocket for him.

DISLIKES Daft buggers in general; Eamon Dunphy and Billy Bingham in particular.

WHAT HE SAYS "Up yours"; "How much will I get?"; "Would your grandmother be Irish by any chance?".

A GUIDE TO THE WORLD CUP SONGS

The World Cup song is an important part of every tournament, and each country has its own style...

EUROPE

Northern European countries such as Germany and Norway have long traditions of aggression, and are terribly boring. Their songs tend to concentrate on conquests, and incorporate dreadful marching music:

We will win; we must win; winning is very important;
If we don't win, we'll be very upset, oh yes.

(Happily, in their own tongues these lyrics do at least rhyme, sometimes.)

Southern Europeans, like the Spanish and Italians, are a more lively people, and their songs — which use Latin rhythms — focus on the romance of the game. This is also the home of the word "Olé".

We love soccer and women too; we like to score with both;
We will cry if we win or lose, and then we'll have a party.

SOUTH AMERICA

The fans here are impoverished, and have nothing in their lives except soccer. As a result, the songs are highly emotional, usually overlaid with a rumba beat:

We have no homes and no money, but we love football;
The World Cup gives us hope, and Maradona is God.

NORTH AMERICA

The USA is the home of cheerleaders, fast cars, and crap soccer teams. The songs are usually lacking in content, like their food:

Rah, Rah, we're the USA; Rah, Rah, Rah, USA OK!!!
  (repeat to fade)

AFRICA

Drums play an important part in African music, due to the scarcity of electric guitars, and electricity generally. The songs concentrate on their athletic prowess, but years of suffering has made the Africans a very realistic people, and the songs usually reflect this:

We're very fast, and the Olympics are our game;
The World Cup isn't.

ASIA

There is very little good to say about Asian music. It is particularly hard on the ear and involves much incomprehensible wailing:

Allah be praised; Aye, Aye, Aye;
May He help us score; Aye, Aye, Aye.

RAY & CHIPS' WORLD CUP SONG

to be sung in rap ...
or whatever you're having yourself

CHORUS:
>We're off, we're off, to Americay
>On one big flamin' holiday
>We're dressed in green
>Tho' we're in the red
>Won't be July
>'til we're back in bed

>Well me name is Ray
>(and my name is Chips)
>We've got our visas
>and our Tayto crisps
>We hit the big Apple in the afternoon
>and they took us to the customs room

>There yer man says to me
>"Anything to declare"
>I tells him straight —
>"Me love for football ...
>... and 600 John Player!"

A few minutes later
Me old pal Jack
Goes up to a cop, to ask
"Where's the crack?"
The last we saw him
He was off to jail
Just another hundred dollars
An' he'll be out out on bail

CHORUS

We were headin' for the match
So we hailed a taxi
When he went up a one-way
I cried "Oh God, we're up the jacksie!"
Then crashin' through a red light
With the sound of sirens buzzin'
We copped who the driver was:
Eamon Dunphy's cousin!

CHORUS

We went into a shebeen
Near 42nd Street
Where everyone was laughin'
And the pints were oh so sweet
Our Jim was on guitar
Until the bouncers caught 'im
Playin' Paddy Reilly
And blow football with his bottom.

(By Graeme Keyes)

THE DUNPHY FACTOR

THE LINE-UP The RTE team of Bill O'Herlihy, Johnny Giles, and Eamon Dunphy is a tight outfit that has remained unbeaten in recent years, thanks mainly to appalling international competition from the likes of "Saint and Greavsie" (the "Cannon and Ball" of TV soccer) and Jimmy Hill.

BACKGROUND The midfield of Giles and Dunphy first built up a reputation during schoolboy Subbuteo competitions with their critical analysis. Dunphy in particular made many enemies, including a young Dick Spring, whom he referred to as "a bollox" after Spring switched sides at half time. He often expressed his outrage by flinging a pencil case, or even his geometry set, across the classroom.

BILL O'HERLIHY The addition of the stylish Bill O'Herlihy brought some much-needed balance to the side. Once described by Dunphy as a good anchorman, but not a great one, his form has been consistent, although the recent debacle involving a champagne bottle suggests that he does not play well under pressure.

STRATEGY They operate a simple 1 - 1 - 1 formation, with O'Herlihy distributing the initial pass to Giles, whose curt style ensures that Dunphy gains possession with plenty of time to spare. Dunphy is the driving force of the team, although he is often erratic, and can attempt to drive a point home — especially late at night — when he would have been better advised to leave it behind and walk. He has recently suffered a loss in form, and is finding it difficult to get back in the driving seat.

"IT'S EITHER EAMON'S POST-MATCH ANALYSIS...
OR THE CABLE HAS GONE AGAIN!"

ITALIA '90 The team hit its peak for Italia '90, when the familiar cry of "hold it there" was timed to perfection during some particularly tricky action replays. However the squiggly white lines that filled our TV screens during half-time often lacked subtlety, while Dunphy almost got his marching orders after recklessly throwing his pen across the studio. Since then he has been become synonymous with the sausage — thanks to Roddy Doyle — and the mildest Irish fans use colourful language when discussing his performance.

USA '94 Like Jack Charlton, RTE has been forced to introduce some young blood for USA '94, splitting up the ageing midfield partnership of Dunphy and Giles. RTE plans to bring in foreign analysts who have Irish grandparents, while Zig and Zag are among the surprise substitutes.

Among the other contenders are Eamonn Casey, who will provide expert analysis of the South Americans; Professor Anthony Clare, for his views on the psychological effects of spending every penny you ever earned on three weeks of football; and Daniel O'Donnell, for his insights into Country & Western soccer (as played by America). C&W soccer is renowned for its sad endings.

WORLD CUP QUIZ

1. What brand of pen did Eamon Dunphy throw down after the Egypt game in 1990?

2. The Irish team is:
   (a) 50% Irish;
   (b) 40% Irish;
   (c) 30% Irish.

3. Complete the following sentence:
   Olé, Olé ....

4. Are the Norwegians:
   (a) boring;
   (b) very boring;
   (c) very very boring.

5. True or False:
   (a) Johnny Giles perms his hair.
   (b) Bill O'Herlihy knows a good champagne.
   (c) Billy Bingham is a good loser.
   (d) Jack Charlton wears a fez.

6. What is Diego Maradona's favourite stimulant?

7. What is wrong with the following statements:
   (a) I want Graham Taylor to manage my team.
   (b) I'm putting my money on South Korea.

8. No British teams qualified for the World Cup because:
(a) Their domestic season is too demanding.
(b) The managers lacked decisiveness.
(c) All the decent players have declared for Ireland.

9. Jack Charlton likes to:
(a) Put the opposition under pressure.
(b) Get the ball behind the man.
(c) Go fishing.

10. Ireland has never won the World Cup because:
(a) The domestic league is underdeveloped.
(b) The team does not travel well.
(c) The grandparents rule was overlooked for too long.

11. The combined ages of the Irish squad is:
(a) 1,213 years.
(b) 1,214 years.
(c) 45,696 years.

12. Fill in the blanks:
The World Cup will be won by G _ R _ ANY
Billy Bingham is a _ _ _ _ _ _
Graham Taylor is a complete _ _ _ _ _ _